T0191195

# The Secret of Fall

Written by
John Coy

Illustrated by
Kristen Adam

PUBLISHED BY SLEEPING BEAR PRESS™

On a warm afternoon,
    while you play tag
        with your friends,
leaves above you hold a secret
        as they dance in the breeze.

You jump over roots
that reach far
and deep
and wide
to pull water into trees.

All around you,
leaves absorb sunlight
to turn air and water into sugar
that trees need to grow.

Leaves of different shapes,
sizes, and shades of **GREEN**
feed trees day after day.

But little by little,
as sunlight decreases

and temperatures cool,

changes happen in the trees.

Each one of the green leaves
has been keeping the secret for months.

*Can you guess what it is?*

In the fall, when growth slows,
leaves stop making food,

and only then begin to show
a collection of colors.

Slowly at first,
with a splash of **ORANGE**,

a burst of **YELLOW**,

a rush of **RED**,

a blast of **BROWN**.

Faster now,
on a hillside,

in the park,

colors appear that could not be seen
when they were covered up
by all that feeding, growing green.

As you and your friends
    share your favorite leaves,
        the secret of fall is in your hands.

Leaves show us
what was hidden
underneath all along–

their own, beautiful colors.

# More on Fall

Trees create the food they need through photosynthesis. This extraordinary process, in which plants use sunlight to make food from water and air, sustains life on Earth.

In trees, roots absorb water and minerals from the soil and pull them up through the wood to the leaves like a gigantic straw. At the same time, leaves take carbon dioxide from the air. Sunlight breaks down water molecules to produce the energy to transform the carbon dioxide into glucose and other sugars that trees need to live. This process of photosynthesis takes place in leaves that appear green due to the pigment chlorophyll, which absorbs sunlight and begins the process of converting carbon dioxide into sugars. Each leaf holds millions of these chlorophyll molecules.

Leaves are green in the spring and summer when they are full of chlorophyll. But during the fall in temperate regions, as sunlight lessens and temperatures cool, food making slows, and deciduous trees (trees that lose their leaves annually) pull nutrients from the leaves into their trunks in preparation for winter. The remaining chlorophyll in the leaves breaks down and the green begins to fade. When this happens, some leaves become more red. Other leaves show colors that have been hidden underneath all that green: orange, yellow, and brown—all together, the beautiful colors of fall.

For all who love fall
-John

For my partner, Kevin,
whose love and support make living my dreams possible
-Kristen

Thank you to Dr. Celia Knight, plant science education consultant, and Brian Schwingle, Forest Health Program Coordinator for the Minnesota Department of Natural Resources, for your generous help in understanding the science of photosynthesis and changes in leaves.
-John Coy

### SLEEPING BEAR PRESS™

2395 South Huron Parkway, Suite 200
Ann Arbor, MI 48104
www.sleepingbearpress.com

Printed and bound in China.

10 9 8 7 6 5 4 3 2 1

Library of Congress Cataloging-in-Publication Data

Names: Coy, John, 1958- author. | Adam, Kristen, illustrator.
Title: The secret of fall / written by John Coy; illustrated by Kristen Adam.
Description: Ann Arbor, MI : Sleeping Bear Press, [2024] | Audience: Ages 4-8 | Summary: "The reason why leaves change colors in the fall is explored. Back matter delves into the science behind photosynthesis"—Provided by publisher.
Identifiers: LCCN 2024005249 | ISBN 9781534113053 (hardcover)
Subjects: LCSH: Autumn—Juvenile literature. | Fall foliage—Juvenile literature.
Classification: LCC QB637.7 .C66 2024 | DDC 508.2—dc23/eng/20240326
LC record available at https://lccn.loc.gov/2024005249